Shine Kids, You're Talented, Gifted and Blessed Go Follow Your Dreams!

Ryan Lee Nevins

Illustrations by Kathy Kerber & Brian Mumphrey

Edited by Michael John Bishop

Scripture quotations are from The Holy Bible, English Standard Version® (ESV®), copyright © 2001 by Crossway, a publishing ministry of Good News Publishers. Used by permission. All rights reserved.

Archway Publishing books may be ordered through booksellers or by contacting:

Archway Publishing
1663 Liberty Drive
Bloomington, IN 47403
www.archwaypublishing.com
1 (888) 242-5904

Because of the dynamic nature of the Internet, any web addresses or links contained in this book may have changed since publication and may no longer be valid. The views expressed in this work are solely those of the author and do not necessarily reflect the views of the publisher, and the publisher hereby disclaims any responsibility for them.

Any people depicted in stock imagery provided by Thinkstock are models, and such images are being used for illustrative purposes only. Certain stock imagery © Thinkstock.

ISBN: 978-1-4808-3482-8 (sc)
ISBN: 978-1-4808-3480-4 (hc)
ISBN: 978-1-4808-3481-1 (e)

Print information available on the last page.

Archway Publishing rev. date: 11/23/2016

Dedicated to my Mom and Dad for always doing their best! Feel the hug! 1022 for good luck! And all those who encourage kids to follow their dreams!

Shine kids!
You're talented, gifted and blessed;
You're God's special little children who are simply the best!

Shine kids!
The Amazing Grace from up above
Was inspired to create you out of goodness and love!

Shine kids!
You're the gift of God's dream;
You gleam like a constellation of stars,
The strongest links on our team!

Shine kids!
You're special and unique,
Designed to reach feats and overcome mountain peaks!

Shine kids!
You're God's joy and pride,
Not the bronze,
Nor the silver,
But the gold, so fly!

Shine kids!
You were born with a purpose and
you were all meant to be;
You're like the sun shining bright over the deep blue sea;
You illuminate the universe causing eye's to squint,
Like a hand full of perfect gems, you're mint!

Shine kids!
Listen and take heed;
You're the diamonds in the rough
that we desperately need,
A true rare breed this is why I plead-
And everyone under the sun unanimously agreed...
You're talented, gifted and blessed
so shine kids and go follow
your dreams!

Do what you love to do!

Don't give up!

Go for it!

Believe + Achieve

HAVE FUN!

Do your best!

You can!

Character Virtues

Inspiration - To be called or encouraged by God to follow a dream or a path in life.

Desire - To want something badly; to have a burning ambition to reach a feat or achieve a goal.

Dedication - The discipline to commit oneself to a task and to make sacrifices in order to reach a desired outcome.

Humility - Modest opinion of one's importance.

Gratitude - To appreciate what one has such as family, friends, talents and opportunities.

Confidence - To believe in oneself and one's abilities.

Integrity - To be honest; to have good character and strong moral principles.

Dignity - To take pride in oneself; to have self-respect.

Strength - To be strong; the ability to deal with adversity; to be resilient.

Patience - The ability to wait without getting upset.

Perseverance - The ability to move forward despite setbacks or problems; to have endurance and determination through hard times of struggle.

Support - People who love and care for you and have your best interests in mind such as family, friends, teachers, coaches and clergy.

Intelligence - The ability to reason, understand, comprehend and make sound decisions.

Prudence - To be careful and cautious; wise in making good judgement; wisdom in looking ahead.

Heart - The will to continue to compete and keep moving forward despite being fatigued.

Discipline - To teach and train oneself to obey rules or codes set by oneself or others; training or controlling oneself to obtain personal growth.

Diligence - To work hard consistently.

Self-Compassion - The ability to be understanding, forgiving and kind to oneself despite failures; to be gentle while evaluating one's own progress.

Courage - To be brave, heroic or valiant; to succeed in facing and overcoming one's fears.

Faith - Complete trust in someone or something such as God, yourself or others.

Hope - Having faith that the best outcome of a situation will occur; staying positive in the midst of trouble and difficulty. In times of doubt remember to say to yourself "Nil Desperandum" which is Latin for "Never Despair" because God is always there!

Joy - A feeling of great pleasure and happiness.

De Colores - Spanish for "In Colors". It is also the name of a song that praises the beauty of diversity and simplicity of God's creation. The colors of the rainbow symbolize God has not forgotten you!

The History of Shine Kids

"Shine Kids, You're Talented, Gifted and Blessed Go Follow Your Dreams!", originated from a graffiti piece I created one night in the back of my grammar school in Auburndale, Queens in 2008. At the time I was angry at the people who had a negative effect on my self-esteem and this is how I expressed it. Not too long after I was inspired to write the poem and since then I have carried the "Shine Kids" message through various means to kids or anyone that was pursuing their dreams. Now I hope to reach and help inspire many through this publication so they too can learn to believe in themselves and have the confidence and courage to follow their dreams!

Thank you to God, Jesus, all of the angels, all of the saints and all of the people He placed in my life to help me throughout the years!

Thank you to all of the people who were a part of the "Shine Kids" journey!

Last but not least thank you to all of the people who helped make this dream become a reality!

Aunt Grace, Tim Sappenfield and Archway Publishing, Kickstarter, BL. FRA ANGELICO ARTIST, Fountain House, Videographers- Andrew Breen, Cyrus Daniel Napolitano, Michael Gennarelli-Hamlin, Brendan Heidenreich, Debra Erwin, Christopher Polgar, Erika Roth, Aunt Chris and Uncle Dan Merkle, Lauren M. Woods, Nicole Schlott-Sullivan, Dr. Paul Hokemeyer, Patricia Doering, Janet Barone, Patricia Shannon, Michael Trotta, Joe Bettles, Bernadette Nolan, Matt Balaker, Tom Burns, Ellen Schaefer, Edmond Olszewski, Jean Oswald, Susan DelGiorno, Erik, Theresa Aquillino, Donald DelGiorno, Donnie DelGiorno, Douglas Nastro, Donna J. Nastro, Erin Nastro, Patrick Nastro, Katy Nastro, Brian H. Moeller, George Woods Jr., Gian Carbonara, Chris Briller, John Geldert, Maureen Nevins Ricker, Elizabeth Krischner, SEZ ME, Barbara Nevins, Len Resto, Kate Jane Neal, Casey M. Felago, Mike Zappier, Denise Borusewicz, Daniel Woods, Noreen Crummy, Nathaniel Baker, Susan Kiernan, Joe Lanzillo, Harold J. Corcuera, Victoria Kalesis, Joan Morris, Sean Behrens, Artesprovita, Hilary Neesam, Christopher Rojas, Michael Muth, Kelly Olino, Bill Condon, Chucky "CKAE" Martello, Father Louis Ardillier, Rosita Cadalin, Grace Wasserman, Msgr. Joseph Finnerty, Deacon Joe Catanello, Joe Kirchner, Marisa Tores, Jimmy Giaima, Katherine Hefferman, Mike Moriarty, Jack Morrissey, Scott Nevins, Bobby Nevins and Edward "Popeye" Nevins.

Ryan Lee Nevins

Former professional baseball player, Golden Gloves boxer, New York City marathoner, peer counselor and award winning poet from New York City. Ryan is inspired to help kids through his experiences using poetry and art. He has helped many kids through his volunteer work with organizations such as the St. Kevin Care and Share program, Special Olympics and working with kids on an individual basis. Ryan's dream is to make "Shine Kids" into a foundation so he can help kids follow their dreams! Shinekidsfoundation.com

"Therefore encourage one another and build one another up just as you are doing."
- 1 Thessalonians 5:11

Thy will be done!

Printed in the United States
By Bookmasters